extreme 9 to 5

Managing Editors: Simon Melhuish and Emma Craven
Series Editor: Lee Linford
Research: Jane Purcell
Design: Alan Shiner

Designed and compiled by
Mad Moose Press
for
Lagoon Books
PO Box 311, KT2 5QW, UK
PO Box 990676, Boston, MA 02199, USA

ISBN: 1-904139-01-9

© MAD MOOSE PRESS 2001
Mad Moose Press and Lagoon Books are trade marks of Lagoon Trading Company Limited.
All rights reserved.

No part of this publication may be reproduced, stored in a retrieval system,
or transmitted in any form or by any other means electronic, mechanical,
photocopying or otherwise, without prior permission in writing from the publisher.

www.madmoosepress.com
www.lagoongames.com

extreme 9 to 5

If you thought that your job was tough, perhaps it's time to reconsider.

Extreme 9 to 5 takes a glimpse into the daily working lives faced by thousands of everyday people across the globe; people who earn a living (or sometimes not) by risking life and limb.

From battling the elements to battling crude oil fires, these are serious occupations with serious risks attached.

Whether it's extremes of temperature, height, depth, speed or stress, or simply life-threatening responsibility, you'll find more than enough reasons to be thankful for a somewhat safer vocation.

space

invaders

star employees

danger rating ●●●●●●●●

ASTRONAUT

ASTRONAUT

salary: US$39,000 - US$78,000

occupational hazards:
- Catastrophic launch failure - estimated risk is 1 in 428.
- Cosmic radiation - one dose equivalent to 100s of chest x-rays.
- Immune system suppression caused by lack of gravity.

training/qualifications:
- Pilot: minimum 1000 hours jet aircraft flight time.
- 3000 applicants every 2 years. 100 selections for testing. 17 selected for further training (0.5%).

fact file:
- 1986: The Challenger Space Shuttle exploded after take-off. All 7 crew were killed. Cause attributed to rubber seals on booster segments that had become inflexible in the cold, allowing explosive gases to leak.

jump suit

caught on camera

danger rating ●●●●●●●●○○

STUNTMAN

salary: US$1000 - US$3000/day

occupational hazards:
- Increasing risks in real stunt work to compete with digital effects.
- Fire/pyrotechnics stunts particularly hazardous.

training/qualifications:
- No official training necessary.
- Most stuntmen qualified in martial arts, stunt driving and riding.

fact file:
- Jackie Chan movies are uninsurable - the actor performs his own stunts.
- Pearl Harbor, the movie, featured the biggest ever single stunt effect involving 30 stuntmen and the blowing up of 6 ships.
- The US has 12,000 registered stuntmen.

extreme working pressure

deep concentration

danger rating ●●●●●●●●●●

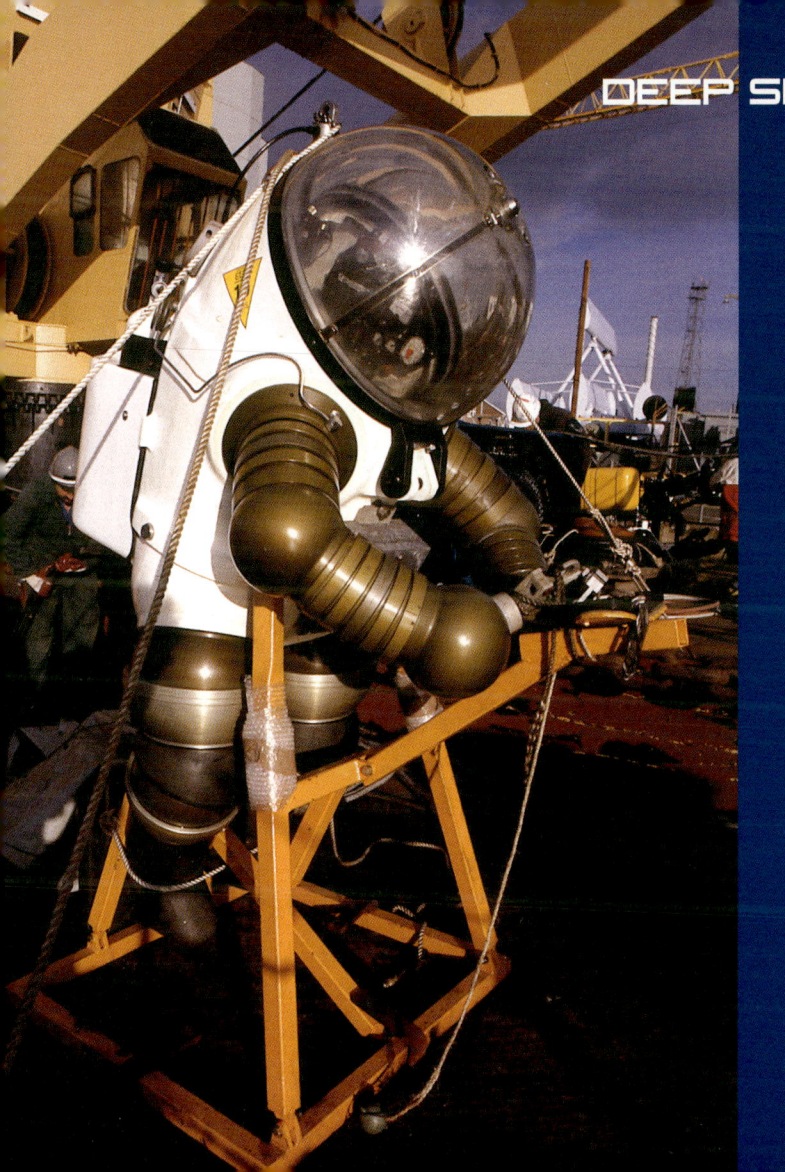

DEEP SEA DIVER

15

DEEP SEA DIVER

salary: US$18,000 - US$35,000

occupational hazards:
- Nitrogen narcosis: excessive nitrogen intake under pressure has an intoxicating effect and causes irrational behavior.
- Decompression sickness (the bends). Causes disorientation, abdominal pain and vomiting. Can result in paralysis or death.
- 21% of diving fatalities are due to rapid ascent or oxygen expenditure.

training/qualifications:
- 2 years training.
- Commercial diver certification.

fact file:
- Atmosphere armored (Jim) suits enable divers to work at depths of 2000ft. Atmospheric pressure at this depth is 0.5 ton.
- The Aquarius underwater lab, Florida Keys, houses scientists for up to 10 days at a time, 60ft below sea level.

streets ahead

every hour is rush hour

danger rating ●●●●●●●●○

salary: US$150/day (minus US$40 lease & US$20 gas)

occupational hazards:
- On average 3,892 New York taxi drivers are robbed each year.
- Around 40 are murdered each year.
- 40% quit within 3 years - violence, stress and struggling to 'make the knot' (break even) are key contributing factors.

training/qualifications:
- 10 days mandatory training with final exam. 70% pass rate.
- Full US driver's license. Fingerprint check.

fact file:
- New York taxi drivers cover 180 miles on an average 12 hour shift.
- 43% of new recruits are from Bangladesh, India or Pakistan.
- New York City has 40,000 taxi drivers.

burning ambition

damage limitation

danger rating ○○○○○○○○○

salary: US$27,000 - US$52,000

occupational hazards:
- Backdraft - explosive fireball caused when a rush of air encounters an oxygen-starved fire - often occurring when a door is opened.
- Flashover - sudden and rapid spread of fire resulting when heat intensity reaches a critical level.
- Smoke inhalation and toxic fumes given off by burning substances.
- Fire-weakened structures present risk of collapse.
- Intense working stress and physical overexertion.

training/qualifications:
- 10-20 weeks training, including paramedics and hydraulics.
- 6 months probation. Continuous testing and evaluation.

fact file:
- Annually, fire destroys $8.6bn worth of property in the US.
- 23% of fires start in the kitchen.

team building

building

tough at the top

danger rating ●●●●●●●●○○

SKYSCRAPER CONSTRUCTION WORKER

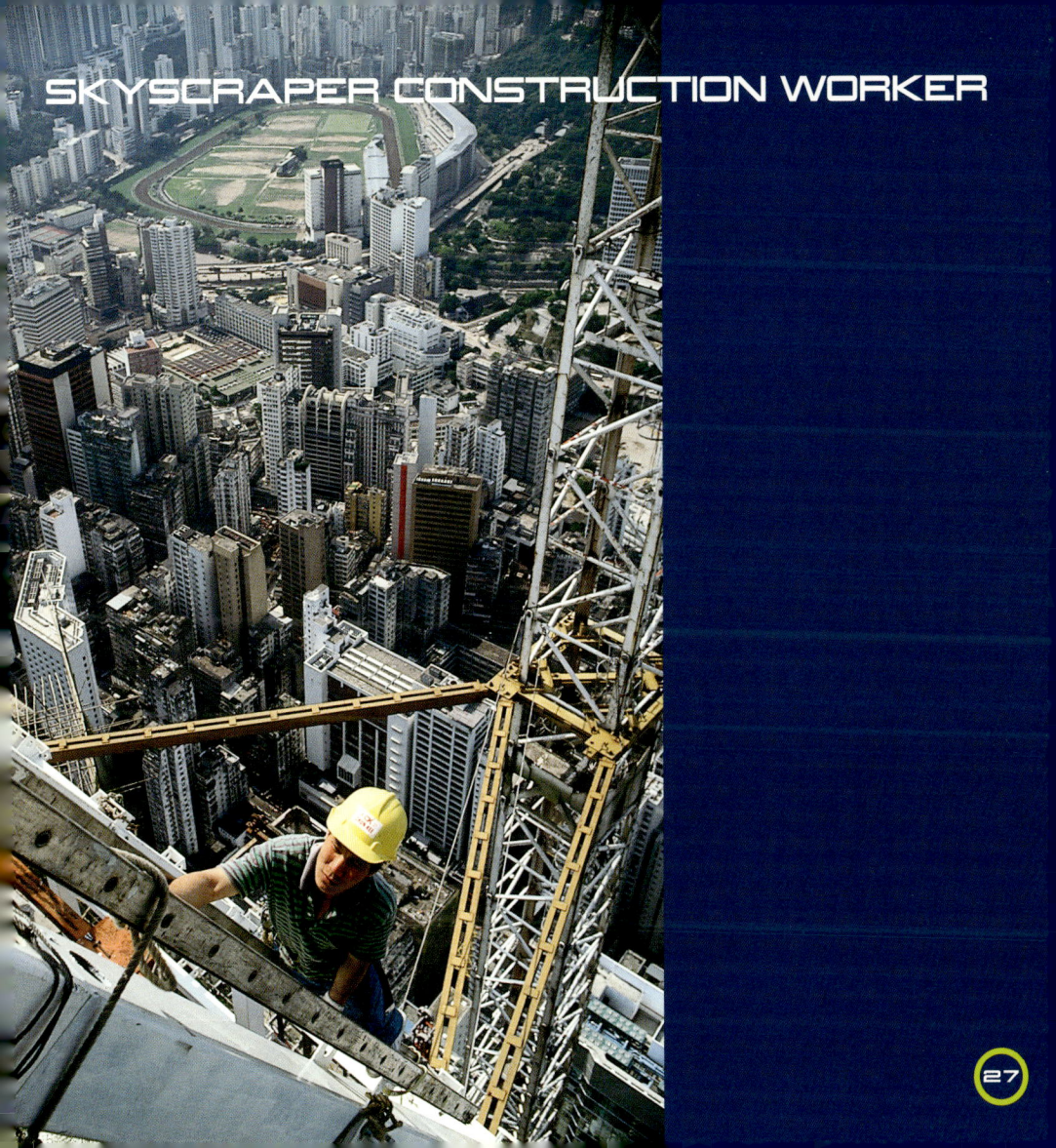

27

- The Sears Tower, Chicago, standing at 1,454 ft, is the tallest building in the US. The CN Tower, Toronto, reaches to 1,815ft and the Petronas Towers, Malaysia, stand at 1,483ft.
- 7 people died during the Empire State Building's construction - 6 workers and a passing pedestrian.

icy

reception

cold and calculated

danger rating ●●●●●●●●○

POLAR PILOT

POLAR PILOT

salary: US$72,000

occupational hazards:
- Severe weather accounts for 44% of all polar aviation fatalities.
- Frequent blind landings (200ft/second) on snow and ice.
- Dehydration - a more serious problem than in the Sahara Desert. The body can lose a gallon of water in one day, the air being too cold to retain moisture.

training/qualifications:
- Commercial pilot's license.

fact file:
- Giant heaters are used to prevent aircraft engines from freezing solid when on the ground.
- Antarctica's average temperature is -17°C. The coldest temperature recorded is -90°C; wind chill can lower temperatures beyond -140°C.
- Antarctica is the world's highest, driest, windiest and coldest continent.

bang
on time

defusing the situation

danger rating ●●●●●●●●●

BOMB DISPOSAL EXPERT

35

- Terrorist car bomb detonation is frequently timed to coincide with the estimated arrival of a bomb disposal team.
- Pipe bomb shrapnel travels at 3000ft/sec. and can kill from 300ft away. Some explosives detonate at up to 30,000ft/sec.

training/qualifications:
- Explosive Ordnance Disposal School (US).
- 25% graduation rate.

fact file:
- LAIRD (Locate, Access, Identify problem, Render safe, Dispose) is the recognised international explosives disposal system.
- Kosovo has the highest number of unexploded bombs in the world - an estimated 11,000 cluster bombs remain from the conflict.

37

the great cold rush

frozen assets

danger rating ●●●●●●●●●

ALASKAN CRAB FISHERMAN

ALASKAN CRAB FISHERMAN

salary: up to US$10,000/month

occupational hazards:
- Environment - 50mph winds, 20-30ft waves.
- Sub-zero temperatures - sea spray can freeze instantly on deck; submergence in icy waters can kill in seconds.
- Exhaustion. Short seasons + big profits = skippers working up to 4 days without sleep.
- Air colder than water can cause heavily laden boats to ice up, destabilize and sink in minutes.

training/qualifications:
- Frequently inadequate. Use of untrained college students criticized by the Occupational Health & Safety Administration.

fact file:
- The industry's fatality rate is 30 times higher than any other in the US.
- In 1999 the Alaskan crab fishing industry netted $190m; the fishing fleet consists of around 220 vessels.

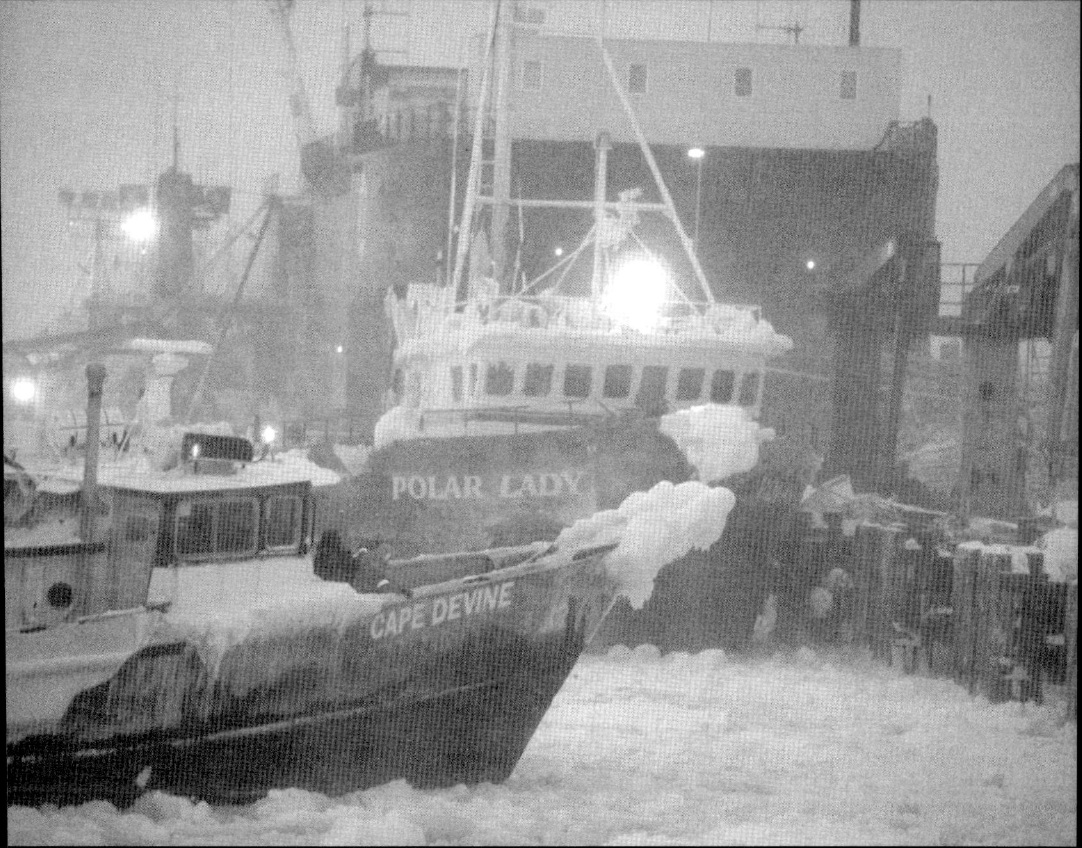
POLAR LADY
CAPE DEVINE

blues brothers

life of crime

danger rating

POLICE OFFICER (SOUTH AFRICA)

salary: US$950/year

occupational hazards:
- Violent crime - 1000 officers have been murdered since South Africa became a democracy in 1994.
- Every 17 seconds a serious crime is committed in the country, Johannesburg being the epicentre.
- Car-jacking is rife. Drivers are resorting to pedal operated, jet-fueled flame throwers as protection. They are currently legal.

training/qualifications:
- Basic 6 months academy training.

fact file:
- 25% of the South African police force are illiterate.
- 40% of the force are black, but just 3 of the country's 53 police generals are black.

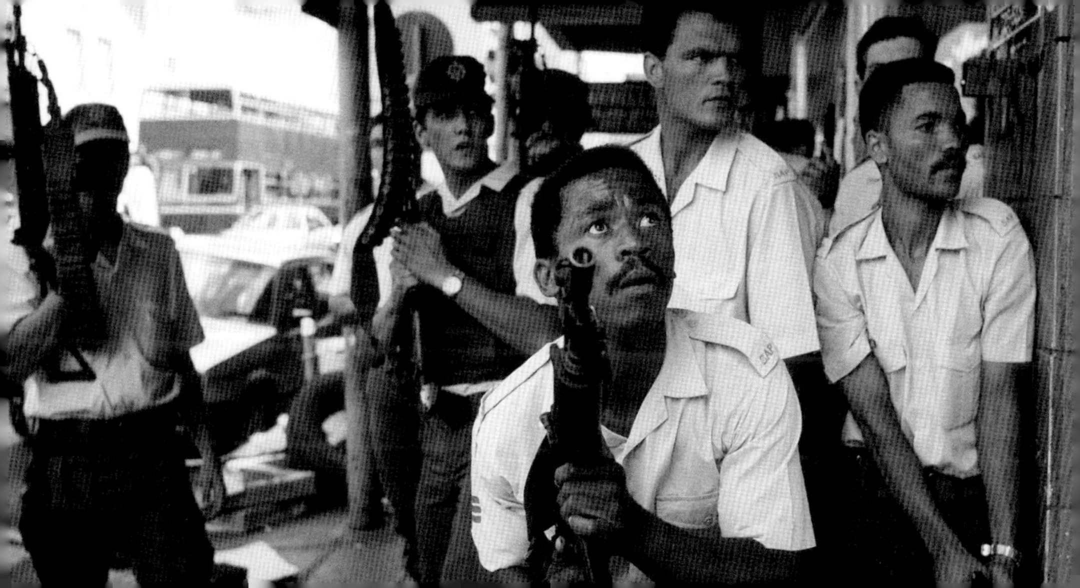

workFlow

heat of the moment

danger rating ●●●●●●●●●

VOLCANOLOGIST

VOLCANOLOGIST

salary: US$30,000 - US$100,000

occupational hazards:
- Collecting lava samples - lava can reach 3,700°C in temperature and flow at 60mph.
- Choking ash and gas clouds (pyroclastic clouds), reaching up to 900°C, traveling at over 100mph.
- Acid rain: sulphuric acid forms when volcanic ash and water droplets mix.
- Volcanic mudflows (lahars) moving at 20-50mph.

training/qualifications:
- PhD in Geology - 8 yrs study.

fact file:
- In 1991, 43 people, including 3 volcanologists, were killed in Japan when Mt. Unzen erupted unexpectedly.
- There are just 300-500 volcanologists in the world today.
- Mt. Krakatoa, Indonesia, saw the world's worst eruption in 1883, triggering a 140ft tsunami. The total death toll reached 36,000.

49

short circuit

line manager

danger rating ●●●●●●●○

F1 RACING DRIVER

51

F1 RACING DRIVER

salary: up to US$40,000,000

occupational hazards:
- High speed collision - F1 cars are capable of exceeding 200mph. Ayrton Senna was tragically killed in 1994 when he crashed at over 180mph.
- Fire - Niki Lauda sustained 1st degree burns at the 1976 German Grand Prix when his car burst into flames.
- Stalling on starting grid - risk of serious collision from rear.

training/qualifications:
- Intense fitness training - Michael Schumacker trains for 4 hours each day to maintain upper body strength.
- Standard 4 hrs training on the day of a Grand Prix.

fact file:
- An F1 driver experiences up to 3gs (gravity force) acceleration.
- Drivers can lose up to 3lbs in sweat during a 70 lap race.
- In F1 history two drivers have plunged into the harbor during the Monaco Grand Prix: Alberto Ascari, 1955 and Paul Hawkins, 1965.

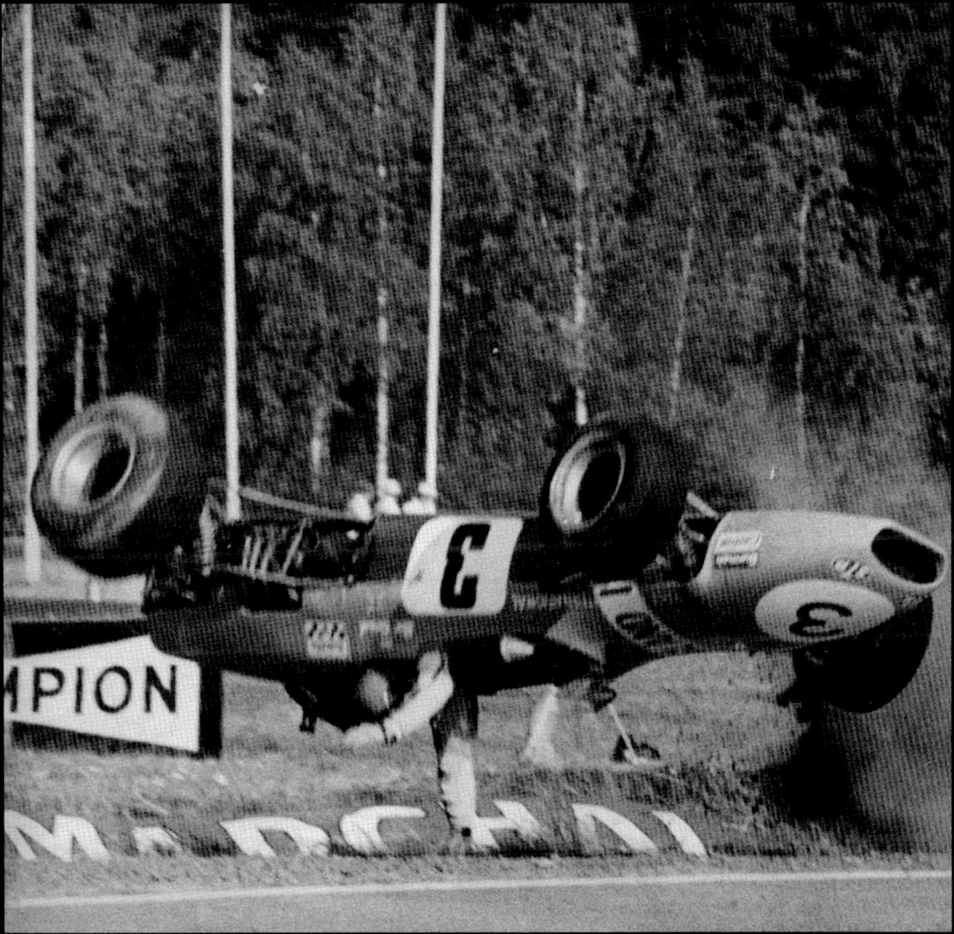
MPION

brush with

danger

paint drops

danger rating ●●●●●●●○○

BRIDGE PAINTER

BRIDGE PAINTER

salary: US$28,000

occupational hazards:
- Falls account for 70% of bridge painting accidents.
- Lead poisoning risk from contact with paint used on older bridges.

training/qualifications:
- Few requirements except for driver's license, high school certificate and ability to work at heights exceeding 300ft.

fact file:
- In 1937 the 'halfway to hell club' was named when 19 bridge painters fell into safety netting under the Golden Gate Bridge.
- The last complete repaint of the Golden Gate took 30 years.
- The Akashi-Kaikyo Bridge, Japan, is the world's longest at 6,532ft.

57

mission
impossible

heroes welcome

danger rating ○○○○○○○○○

PARAJUMPER

PARAJUMPER

salary: Technically volunteers (receiving monthly bonuses)

occupational hazards:
- PJs are dispatched to the world's most politically volatile hotspots.
- Extreme rescue environments: war zones, the Arctic, severe weather.

training/qualifications:
- Selection: 6 weeks boot camp, 10 week indoctrination. 13% succeed.
- 18 months enduring 'The Pipeline': combat training, combat diving, army airborne school, survival, freefall parachuting, specialist recovery, medic training.

fact file:
- Pararescue teams were assembled to recover downed US military aircraft and crews. They also conduct high-risk civilian rescues.
- There are just 400 PJs worldwide, operating in teams of around 30.
- PJs are put on global alert whenever NASA launches a space mission; they rescued Neil Armstrong and David Scott from the Gemini 8 capsule in 1966 when the space mission aborted over the Pacific.
- In 1991, PJs ditched their helicopter in 60ft waves whilst attempting rescue of the Andrea Gail fishing crew - the real life 'Perfect Storm'.

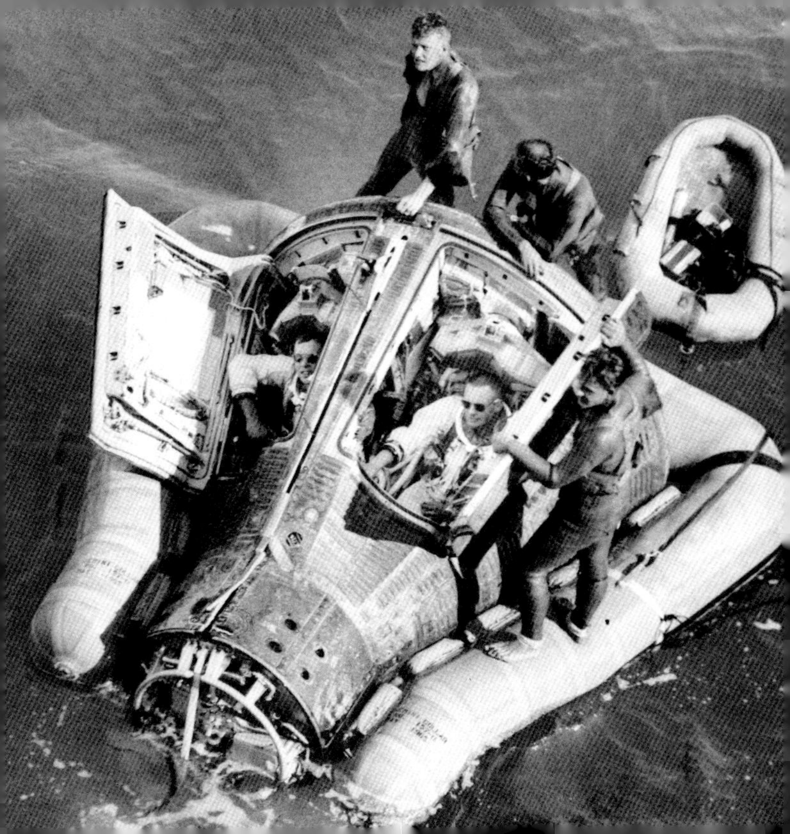

in the line of fire

crude working methods

danger rating ●●●●●●●●●

BLOWOUT CONTROLLER

63

BLOWOUT CONTROLLER

salary: US$500 - US$1000/day

occupational hazards:
- Extreme temperatures - a crude oil blowout can reach 1677°C; common working temperatures are 125°C.
- Toluene exposure - causes liver and kidney damage. Blowout workers may be exposed to 800 times more Toluene than exists in urban air.
- Smoke and toxin inhalation.

training/qualifications:
- Requirements include drilling, engineering and oil well capping.

fact file:
- Crude oil heats and sinks before it can burn off, creating a liquid heatwave; contact with water causes a steam explosion that can shoot 1000ft into the air.
- $60 billion worth of oil was destroyed in Kuwait during the Gulf War. Red Adair (shown right) extinguished 117 of the conflict's 607 oil fires.

65

Fatal extraction

networking skills

danger rating ●●●●●●●●

MINER

67

MINER

salary: US$50,000 (US$18,000 in South African gold mines)

occupational hazards:
- Rockfall and rockbursts - South African gold mines riskiest due to depth (up to 3km), higher explosive requirements and brittle rocks.
- Pneumoconiosis (black lung) and asbestos poisoning.
- Tuberculosis - 4000 miners develop the disease each year.
- High cancer risks associated with Uranium ore mining.
- Dangerous gases, dust and poor air quality.
- Fire: 91 miners died in Idaho, May 1972 when fire broke out 3,700ft below ground.

training/qualifications:
- Minimum 40 hours training.

fact file:
- 250 men die in South Africa's gold mines every year, 6 out of 10 due to rockfall and rockburst.
- The US produces around 1,074,777,945 tons of coal each year.

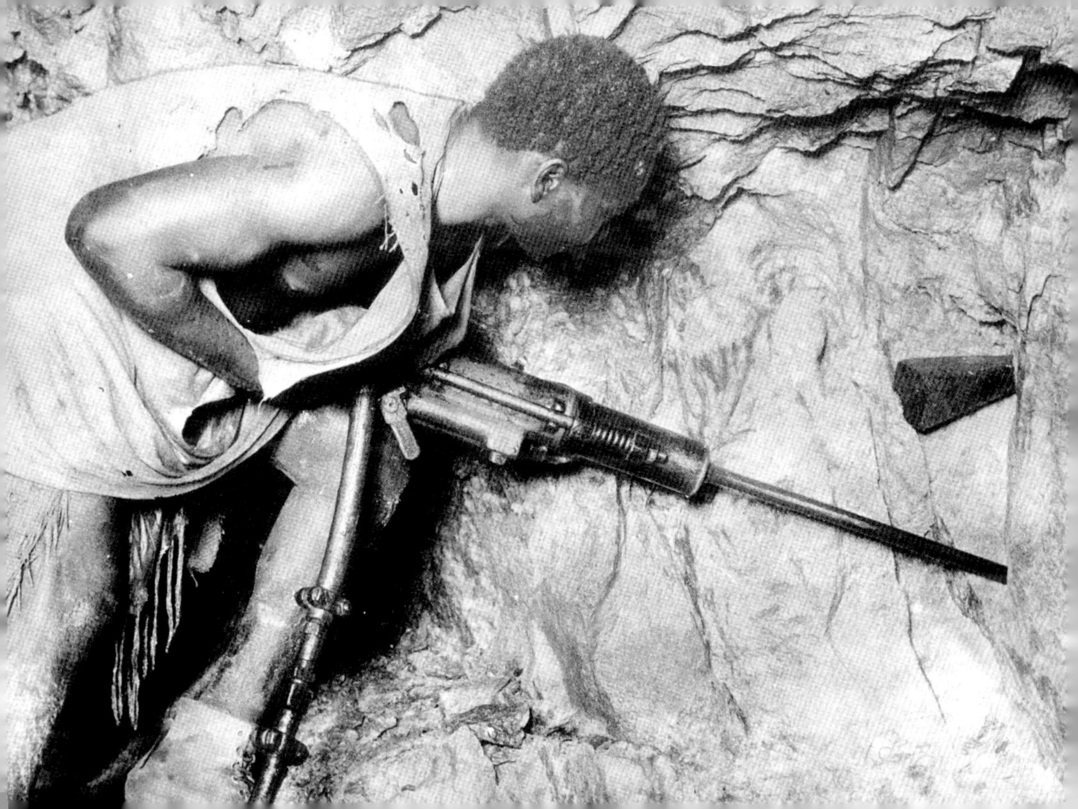

peak

performance

altitude slickness

danger rating

MOUNTAIN RESCUER

71

MOUNTAIN RESCUER

salary: Voluntary

occupational hazards:
- Avalanches account for 30% of all mountain fatalities.
- AMS (Acute Mountain Sickness) - a risk from 10,000ft plus. Symptoms include nausea, dizziness and breathlessness, in severe cases, death.
- Concealed crevasses covered by unstable snowbridges.
- Hypothermia, hypoxia and hypoxemia.

training/qualifications:
- Mountaineering/climbing experience, hiking, forestry & geology skills.
- Mountain Rescue Council (UK) provides 1 day's training per month.

fact file:
- Worldwide, 4000 mountain rescue callouts are made annually. 33% of lost mountaineers are found unharmed.
- Sniffer dogs can trace human scent under as much as 10ft of snow.
- 11 major expeditions are made on Mt. Everest each year. The mountain's mortality rate is 5.8%, 69% due to falls or avalanche

73

snap happy

swamp fever

danger rating ●●●●●●●●○○

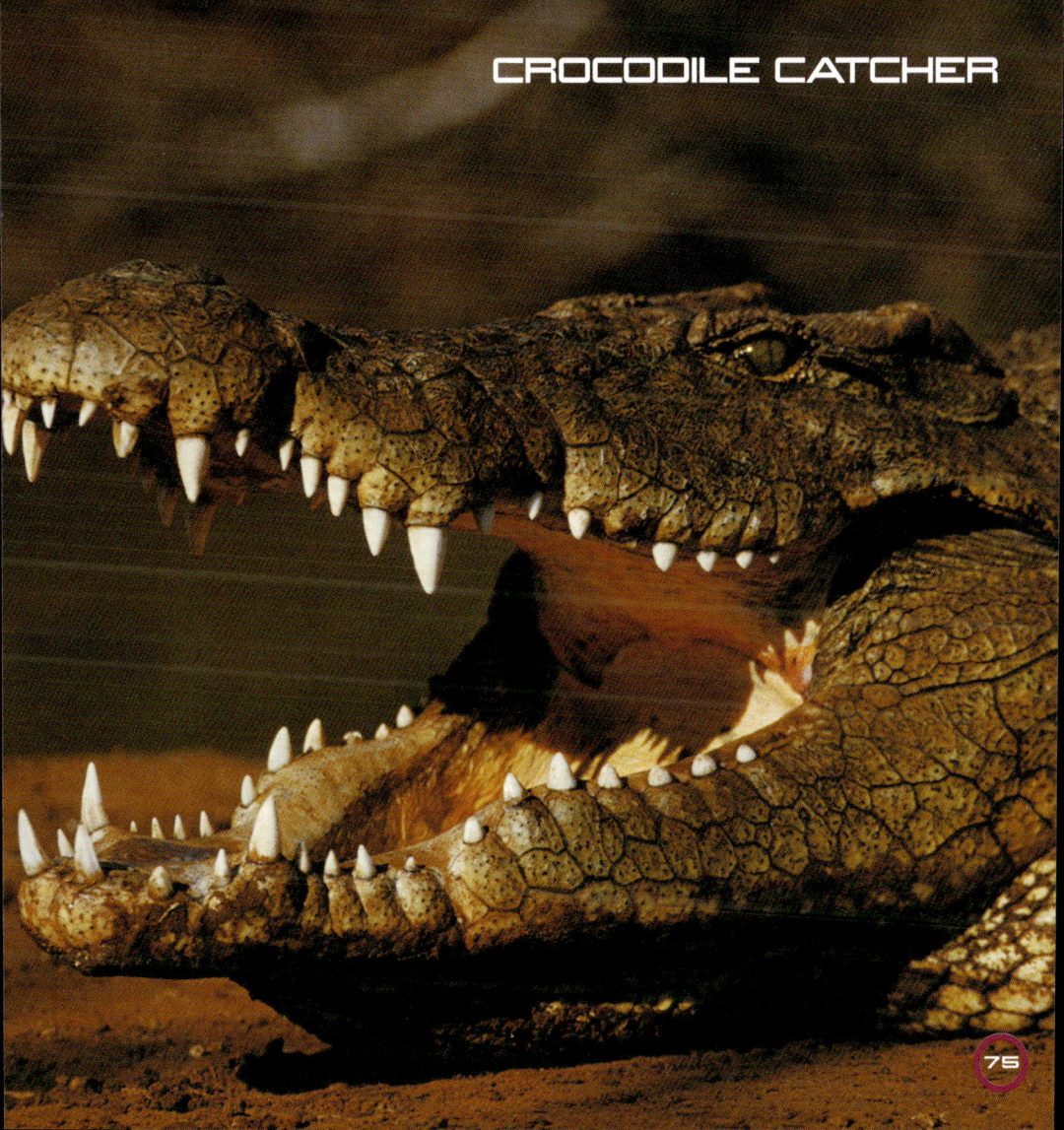

CROCODILE CATCHER

CROCODILE CATCHER

salary: US$30,000 - US$50,000

occupational hazards:
- Speed of attack: a crocodile can launch itself from the water at 43mph.
- Death rolls: crocodiles roll their captives over and over in the water until they drown.
- A single blow from a crocodile's tail can break your legs.

training/qualifications:
- Qualified herpetologists require an MA or PhD in Biology.
- Crocodile catchers need a capture license.

fact file:
- Catchers have to move quickly; crocodiles can run at 18mph for up to 100m. Beyond this distance they are at fatal risk from Lactic Acidosis.
- Crocodiles have remained physiologically unchanged for 200 million years. Males can grow to 20ft long and live for 100 years.

77

juggling act

all along the watchtower

danger rating ●●●●●●●○○

AIR TRAFFIC CONTROLLER

AIR TRAFFIC CONTROLLER

salary: US$50,000 - US$80,000

occupational hazards:
- Severe stress leading to abnormally high instances of peptic ulcers, viral infections and headaches. Retirement age considered at 50.
- Prolonged EMS exposure (radar screens) causing fatigue, additional stress and skin irritation (shifts split into 90 minute blocks).

training/qualifications:
- FAA Air Traffic Control Academy training (US).
- On the job training - full qualification takes several years.

fact file:
- US Air Traffic Control is responsible for 1 billion passengers each year; Atlanta, the world's busiest airport handles 80 million.
- Since 1982 air traffic has increased by 35%; the number of ATCs continues to fall.
- Current aircraft separation standards require 2000ft vertical spacing. Increased traffic and new technology may reduce this to 1000ft.

81

body armor

protection money

danger rating ●●●●●●●○

BODYGUARD

salary: US$400 - US$2000/day

occupational hazards:
- Assassination - Columbia is riskiest with a homicide rate 9 times higher than the US. Political homicide stands at 65%; most Columbian bodyguards work for politicians.
- Violent or obsessive stalkers - US celebrities spend an average of $250,000 per year for protection against them.

training/qualifications:
- Ex-secret service or ex-military training preferred.
- Firearms training essential.

fact file:
- The US has 15,000 bodyguards - demand has doubled in the last 20 years.
- Elvis had a posse of bodyguards called 'The Memphis Mafia'.
- Michael Jackson has 8 bodyguards, Eminem has 50.

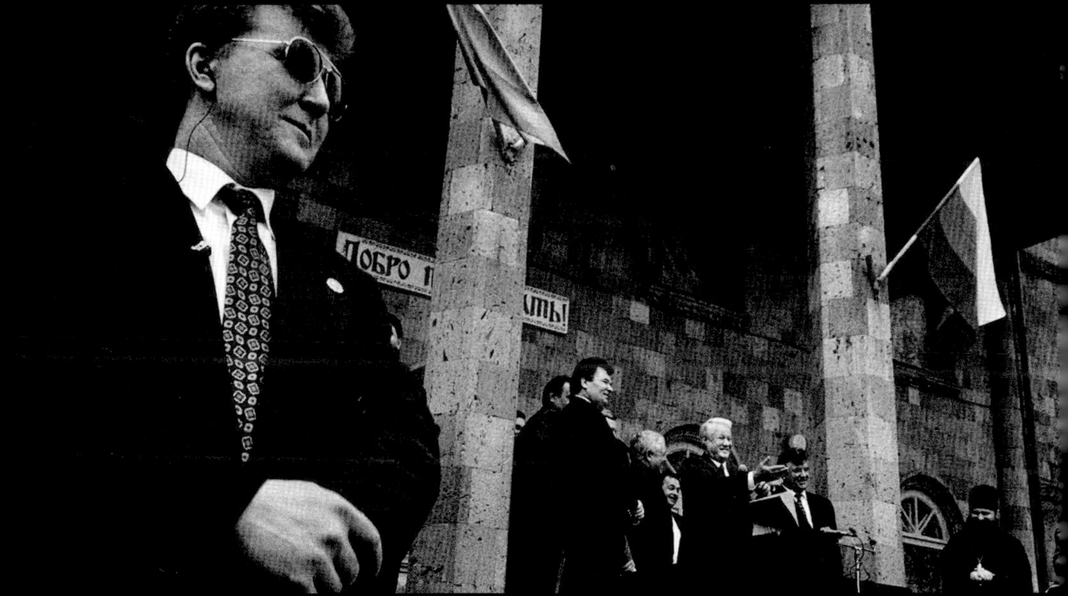
ДОБРО

storm troopers

call to action

danger rating ●●●●●●●●

COASTGUARD

87

COASTGUARD

salary: US$16,500 - US$22,700

occupational hazards:
- Storm force winds exceeding 70mph.
- 60ft waves, bearing down at 50mph weigh 000's of tons.
- Toxic chemical spillage from capsized vessels.

training/qualifications:
- National Lifeboat School (US) - graduation requires a rescue and 360° boat roll in waves up to 15ft.

fact file:
- The RNLI (voluntary UK Coastguard) has saved 132,000 lives since it was set up in 1824.
- The US Coastguard annually responds to 39,000 distress calls and saves around 3,800 lives. In the year 2000 they also seized $4.4bn worth of illegal drugs.

SELSEY LIFEBOAT

join the jet set

cloud base

danger rating ●●●●●●●●●

FIGHTER PILOT

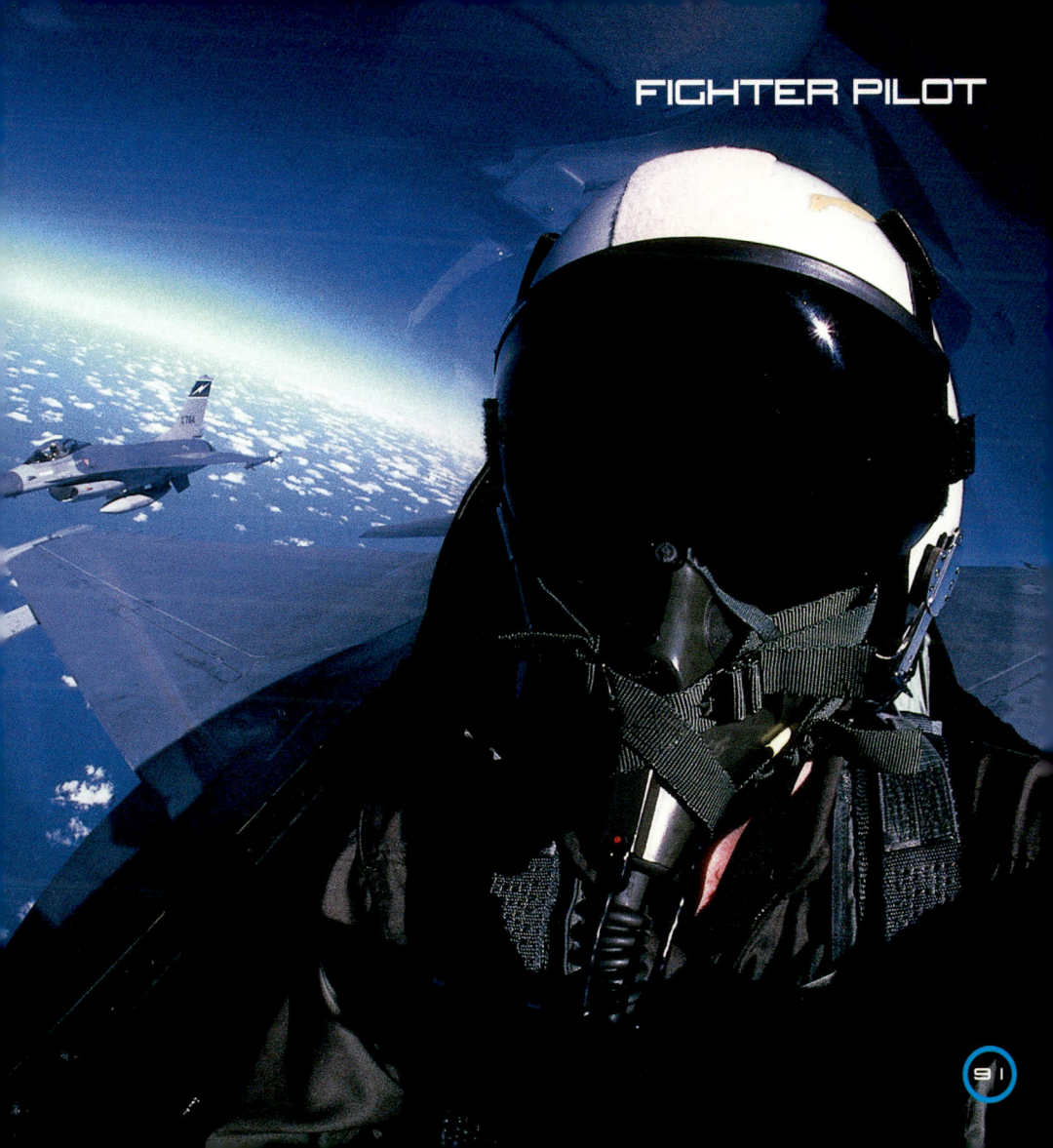

salary: US$30,000 - US$45,000

occupational hazards:
- Extreme gravitational force: 4-6gs can cause blackout in seconds (G-LOC). An F-16 can pull 9gs, fatal without an anti-g suit.
- Disorientation can result in a crash.
- Hypoxia (lack of oxygen at altitude) can kill in 5 seconds at 40,000ft.
- Combat: 38 coalition aircraft were downed during Desert Storm, 400 during the Battle of Britain.

training/qualifications:
- 7 years training (includes 2 years as a wingman).

fact file:
- 168 F-15s flew 8,100 sorties during Operation Desert Storm. Average sortie length was 3-5hrs. Training sorties are usually 1.5hrs.
- The US has 4000 new aircraft on order; the cost is estimated at $350 bn.
- Of Russia's 5,000 military aircraft only 1,600 can be flown.

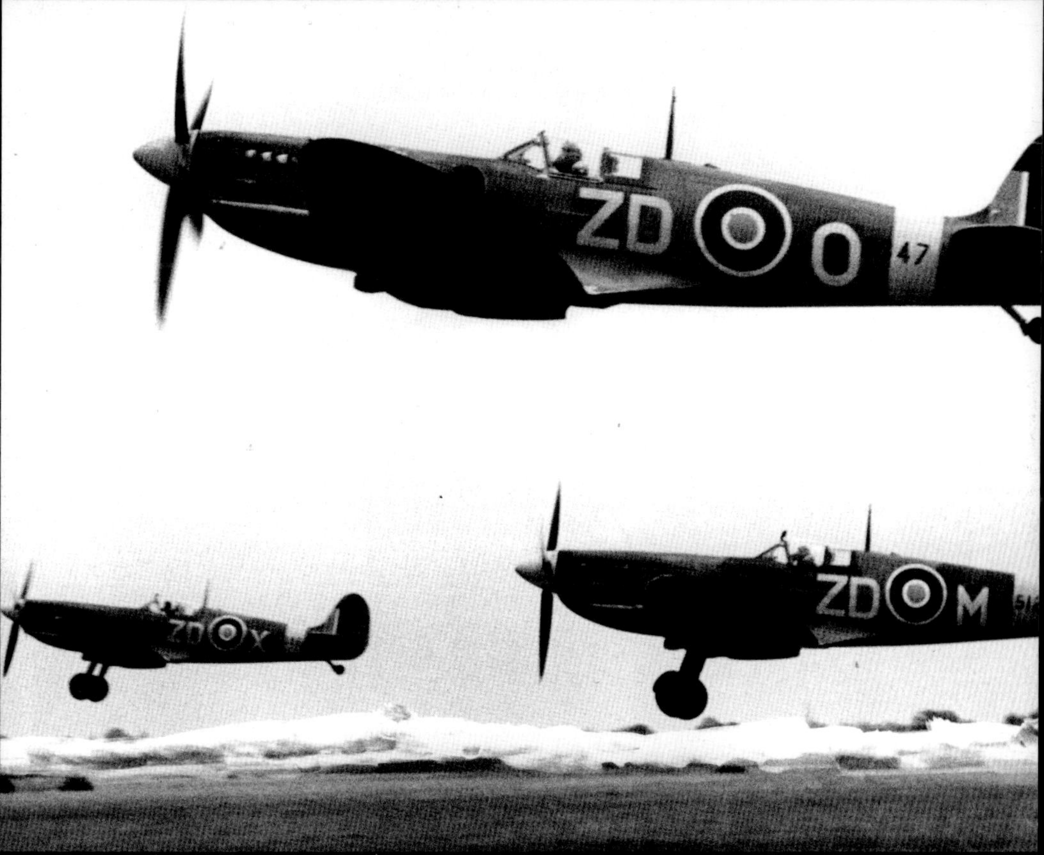
ZD O
47
ZD M
ZD X

Further information and related links.

Astronaut
www.nasa.gov
www.esa.int

Stuntman
www.stuntplayers.com
www.stuntrev.com
www.usastunt.com
www.stuntschool.com

Deep Sea Diver
www.naocd.org
www.diveweb.com
www.padi.com

New York Taxi Driver
www.ny-taxi.com
www.nycabbie.com

Firefighter
www.iaff.org
www.nfpa.org
www.fireservicecollege.ac.uk

Skyscraper Construction Worker
www.skyscraper.org
www.constructioneducation.com
www.agc.org

Polar Pilot
www.antarctica.ac.uk
www.borekair.com
www.alaska.faa.gov/flytoak/Arctic/ARCTIC.HTM
members.tripod.com/PolarFlight/historicflights2.htm

Bomb Disposal Expert
www.army-rlc.co.uk
www.ngeod.com
www.atra.mod.uk/atra/RSME/DEOD
www.cnet.navy.mil/eods/command/index2.html

Alaskan Crab Fisherman
www.cfec.state.ak.us
www.cdqdb.org/group/cbs/cbshome.htm
www.nationalfisherman.com

Police Officer (South Africa)
www.saps.org.za
www.crimeresearch.org.za

Volcanologist
www.soest.hawaii.edu/GG/hcv.html
www.eos.pgd.hawaii.edu
www.iavcei.org

F1 Driver
www.f1-live.com
www.sports.com/f1

Bridge Painter
www.fhwa.dot.gov
www.highways.gov.uk

Parajumper
www.specialtactics.com

Blowout Controller
www.redadair.com

Miner
www.infomine.com
www.northernminer.com
www.mining-technology.com

Mountain Rescue Worker
www.mountain.rescue.org.uk
www.mra.org

Crocodile Catcher
www.flmnh.edu/natsci/herpetology

Air Traffic Controller
www.natca.org
www.nats.co.uk
www.faa.gov
www.caa.co.uk

Bodyguard
www.ibabodyguards.com
www.bodyguards-pba.com

Coastguard
www.mcga.gov.uk
www.uscg.mil
www.rnli.org.uk

Fighter Pilot
www.af.mil
www.raf.mod.uk
www.raf-careers.com
www.usaf.com

Images reproduced with the kind permission of:

Getty Images

Corbis Images

Sylvia Cordaiy PL/Nigel Rolstone & Johnathan Smith

Skyscan Photolibrary/Chris Allan & John Farmar

Travel Ink/Derek Allan

Ace Photo Agency:
Benelux Press/Fotopic/Peter Walton Photography

Network Photographers/Anthony Suau & P Velasco

British Antarctic Survey/Andy Alsop

Accent Alaska/Daryl Kyra Lee

Syndication International

Firepix International

The Stunt Company (South Africa)

Other titles in the range include Extreme Sports.

Printed in Hong Kong